Electricity

Where Does It Come From? Where Does It Go?

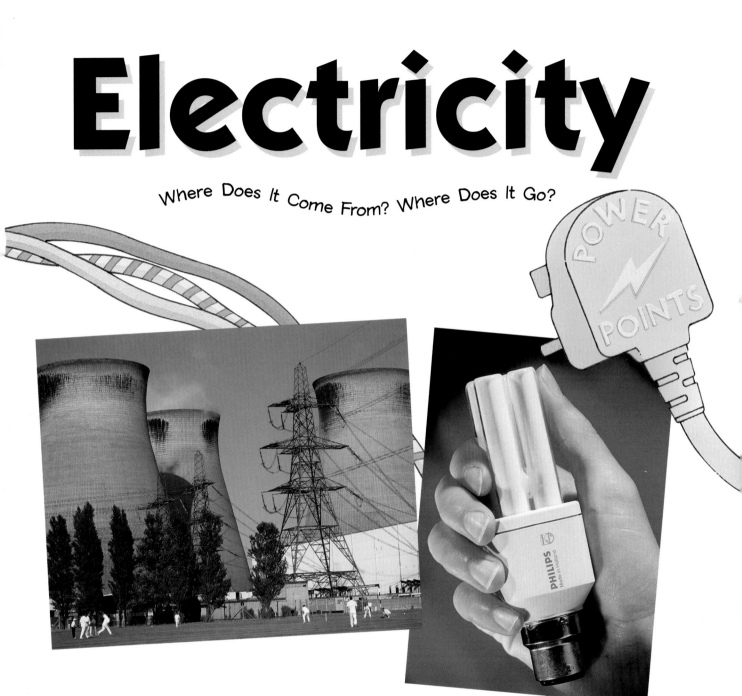

Paul Humphrey

Photography by Chris Fairclough

FRANKLIN WATTS

LONDON•SYDNEY

© 2000 Franklin Watts

First published in Great Britain by
Franklin Watts
96 Leonard Street
London
EC2A 4XD

Franklin Watts Australia
56 O'Riordan Street
Alexandria
NSW 2015
Australia

ISBN: 0 7496 3921 0
Dewey Decimal Classification 621.31
A CIP catalogue record for this book is available from the British Library

Printed in Malaysia

Planning and production by Discovery Books
Editors: Tamsin Osler, Samantha Armstrong
Design: Ian Winton
Art Director: Jonathan Hair
Illustrators: Stuart Trotter, Raymond Turvey
Commissioned photography: Chris Fairclough

Acknowledgements
Franklin Watts would like to thank the following for their help in the production of this
book: British Nuclear Fuels, Edison Mission Energy, National Power, NPower and Seeboard.
The photograph on page 15 (bottom) was kindly supplied by Bruce Coleman
(Neil McAllister).

Contents

Switch on the light!

Look around you. You are surrounded by things that use electricity. Electric lights let you see when it is dark.

Electric clocks tell you when it is time to wake up in the morning and when to go home from school.

Our homes are full of electrical gadgets, from toasters and microwaves to computers and playstations. Our central heating systems may be powered by electricity too.

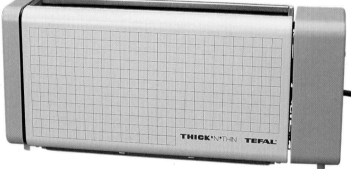

Some small, portable gadgets, like torches and personal stereos are powered by batteries that only last for a few hours. Then they need to be replaced or recharged.

But the electricity that comes from the sockets on the wall is there *all* the time, at the flick of a switch. Where does it come from?

Why 'electricity'?

Electricity gets its name from 'electron', the ancient Greek word for amber. The Greeks discovered that by rubbing a piece of amber with a silk cloth they could make it pick up dust and scraps of straw. This type of electricity is called static electricity.

Electricity meters

Electricity enters your home through one thick underground cable or an overhead wire. It goes to a service board or consumer unit. Here you will find the main switch. If the electricity supply to your home needs to be turned off, this would be done at the main switch.

Sometimes the electricity meter is also here, or it may be outside. Have a look for your meter — try looking under the stairs or in an outside cupboard. The meter has clock faces or a set of numbers that tell you how much electricity you use.

A wheel turns round and round inside the meter when electricity is being used. The more electricity being used, the faster the wheel turns round.

Every three months or so, a meter reader comes to read the meter. Then you get a bill showing how many 'units' of electricity you have used and how much you have to pay.

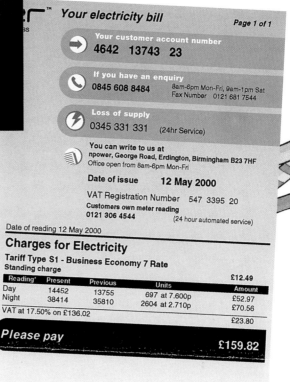

Your electricity bill

Page 1 of 1

Your customer account number
4642   13743   23

If you have an enquiry
0845 608 8484
8am-6pm Mon-Fri, 9am-1pm Sat
Fax Number   0121 681 7544

Loss of supply
0345 331 331   (24hr Service)

You can write to us at
npower, George Road, Erdington, Birmingham B23 7HF
Office open from 8am-6pm Mon-Fri

Date of issue   **12 May 2000**

VAT Registration Number   547 3395 20
Customers own meter reading
0121 306 4544   (24 hour automated service)

Date of reading 12 May 2000

Charges for Electricity

Tariff Type S1 - Business Economy 7 Rate
Standing charge   £12.49

Reading*	Present	Previous	Units	Amount
Day	14452	13755	697 at 7.600p	£52.97
Night	38414	35810	2604 at 2.710p	£70.56
VAT at 17.50% on £136.02				£23.80

Please pay   £159.82

★ Meter Reading key applies:
E = Estimated, C = Customers own and R = Removed

Your
Supply
Number

S	04	911	010
14	1973	6902	008

Registered Office:Midlands Electricity plc, Whittington Hall, Whittington, Worcester, WR5 9RB Registered in England and
Wales: No. 2366928 . National Power (Energy Co.) Ltd acts as an agent for Midlands Electricity in the supply of electricity.

Making it safe

Electricity is dangerous. If you touch wires carrying electricity, it can kill you. It is very powerful and can cause a fire. Trip switches and fuses help make electricity as safe as possible.

Trip switches automatically cut off the electricity if there is a fault. There are lots of trip switches for different parts of the house.

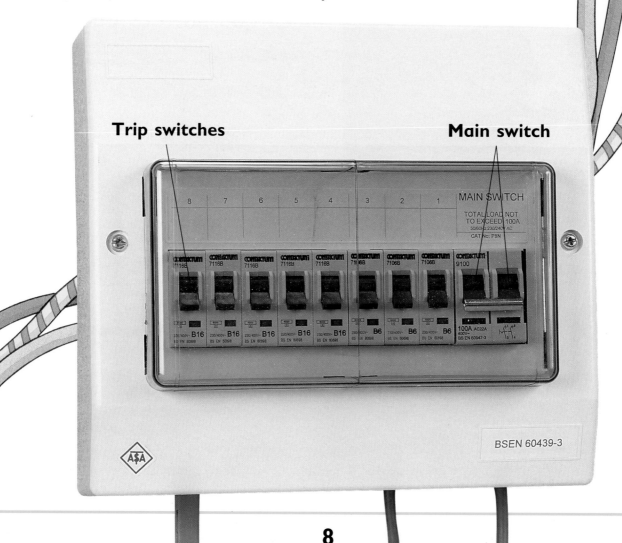

Trip switches

Main switch

The fuses are found in the fuse box.
Ask an adult to show you inside a fuse.
The wire inside gets hot and breaks if
you plug in a faulty lamp or other
appliance. This cuts off the supply
and stops a fire starting.

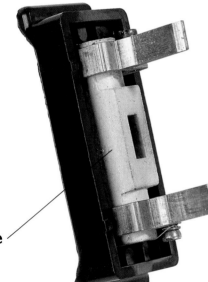

Fuse

Fuse wires have different
thicknesses depending on how much power
an appliance needs. Electric cookers, electric
heating systems and water heaters need a lot
of power, so they have thick fuse wires.
Lights need less so they
have thin fuse wires.

Making a circuit

From the consumer unit, electricity travels around your home in 'mains' circuits. The lights have one circuit, the wall sockets have one, or maybe two circuits, and the electric cooker and water heater have their own circuits.

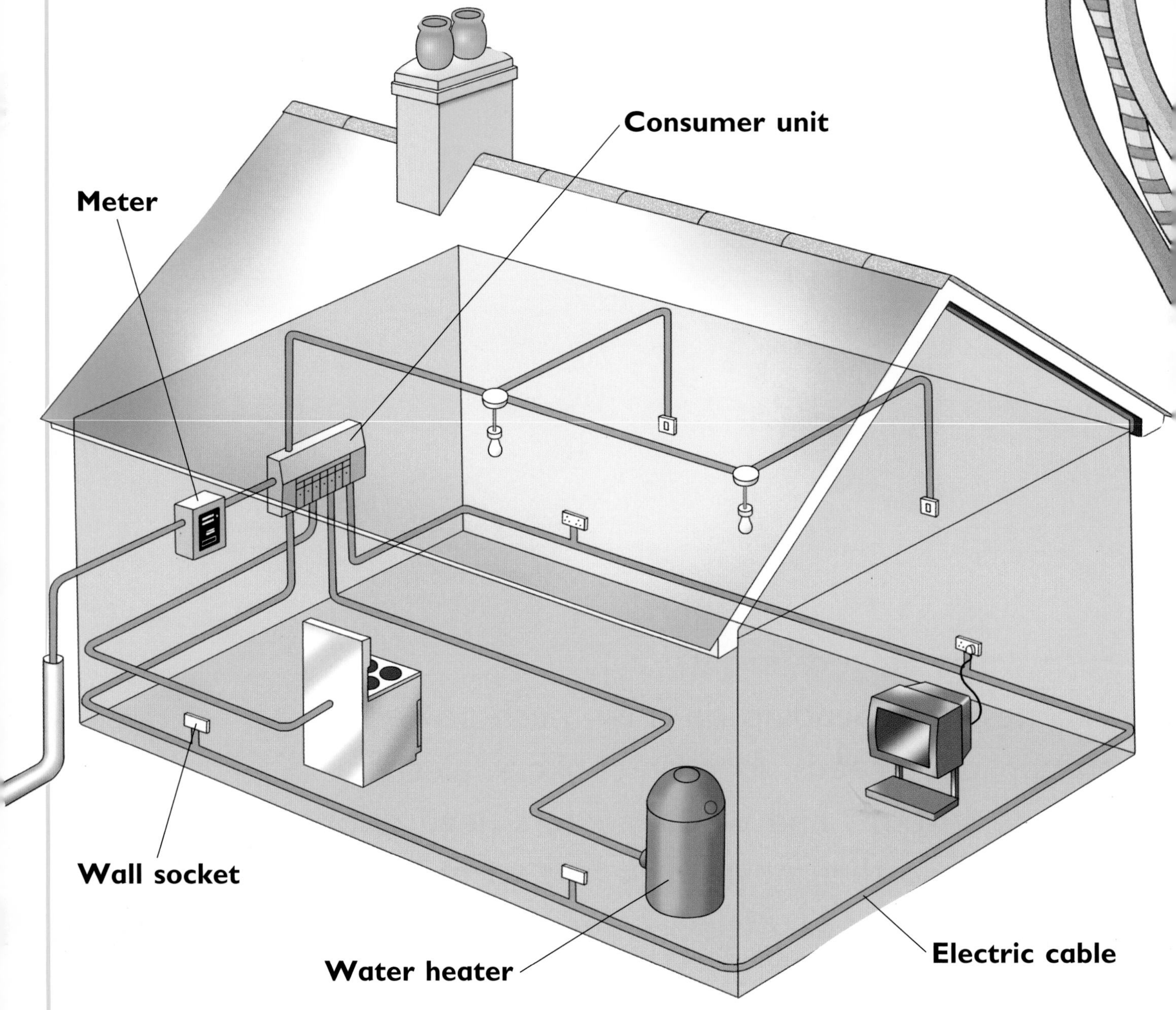

Consumer unit

Meter

Wall socket

Water heater

Electric cable

The electricity travels inside thick white, or grey, cables. These cables lie under the floorboards, in the walls or in the loft. Their white or grey plastic covering acts as an insulator to stop anything coming into contact with the wires. Inside are three thinner cables. Inside each of these cables is a wire carrying your electricity.

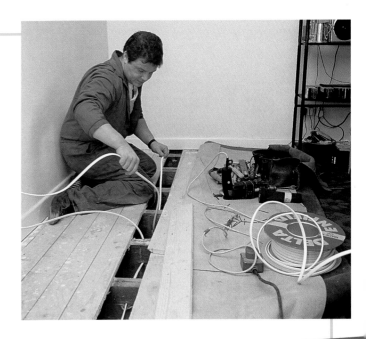

Stored electricity

Perhaps you have made a circuit using a battery and a light bulb. When you connect a battery and a light bulb together with two wires, the bulb lights up. You have made a circuit.

'Mains' electricity from the plug is much more powerful than the 'stored' electricity in a battery. Never make circuits with mains electricity; always use batteries.

Plug it in!

Where you see a light switch or a wall socket, a smaller cable comes off the mains cable and goes into the socket. The three wires in the mains cable are attached to the three holes in the socket.

Ask an adult to show you inside a plug. See the different coloured wires? There is also a little tube. Inside this is a fuse. Like main fuses, this will break if the plug is connected to faulty equipment.

What do the colours mean?

In a plug the brown wire is called the live wire and the blue is the neutral wire. These two wires carry electricity. The green and yellow wire is the earth wire, a safety wire that allows electricity to pass into the ground if your house is struck by lightning.

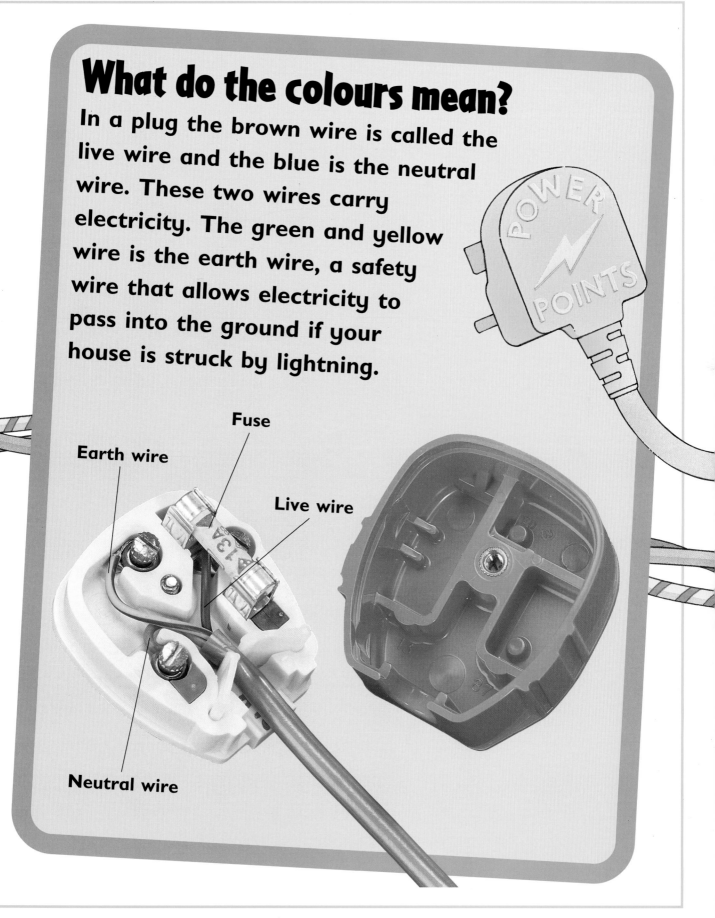

Fuse

Earth wire

Live wire

Neutral wire

At work

Without electricity, our lives would be almost impossible. We rely on it at home and in our factories.

Electric furnaces melt steel, electric robots build cars and our computers and the Internet depend on electricity.

In hospitals, electricity powers the machines that help keep people alive and get better.

Most shops and supermarkets use bar code readers, which scan the black and white stripes on goods. These are linked to computerized cash tills powered by electricity.

Many goods are transported by electric vehicles, and wheelchairs and milk floats can be electrically powered. Even trains depend on electricity, and no planes would get off the ground without it.

Where does it come from? How is it made and how is it transported? It all starts at the power station.

At the power station

These are huge buildings where heat is turned
into electricity. This is called generating electricity.
The heat is made by burning fuel to heat water.

Until recently most power stations in Britain
burned coal. Today there are gas-fired power
stations and nuclear power stations. We also
have oil-fired power stations, and we use
wind and water to generate electricity.

Power stations are usually near the sea or a river
because they use enormous amounts of water.

Nuclear reaction

About a quarter of Britain's electricity is generated in nuclear power stations. Nuclear power is made from a metal called uranium.

Uranium, like all substances, is made up of tiny particles. When the tiny particles in certain types of uranium are split apart, huge amounts of heat are given off. This is called a nuclear reaction.

This is what the inside of a nuclear power station looks like.

Turning the turbines

In coal or oil-fired stations the water is heated by burning coal or oil. In nuclear-powered stations the water is heated by nuclear reaction. The water boils and makes steam which is forced out of the boiler, along pipes. The steam shoots into a huge turbine.

These pictures show the turbine hall of a power station (below) and a turbine (right).

A turbine is a bit like a huge propeller. It turns a machine called a generator, which makes electricity. You may have a generator, called a dynamo, on your bike. As you pedal, the bike wheel turns a dynamo that powers your lights.

Do you have a power station near where you live? The huge towers are called cooling towers. Once the steam has turned the turbines it is cooled in these cooling towers.

Fossil fuels

Coal and oil are called fossil fuels. They are made out of wood and plants that have been in the ground for millions of years. Burning fossil fuels harms our environment. It produces gases which can pollute rain water.

Alternative energy

As well as polluting our environment, the world's coal and oil will run out one day. So electricity companies need to find alternative sources of energy.

One source is the Sun. The Sun's heat and light could be focused onto a small area so that it heats water in a boiler and raises steam just like an ordinary power station.

Another way is to use the wind to turn giant turbines that are joined to electrical generators. The wind is free and it will last for ever. It is called a renewable source of energy.

Hydro-electric power (HEP) means power from water. When a dam is built across a river valley a large lake builds up behind it.

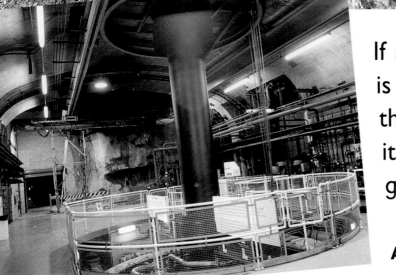

If some of this water is allowed to flow though a turbine it can be used to generate electricity.

An HEP turbine.

Pylons and volts

Now that all this electricity has been made, how does it get to your house?

Electricity companies often use helicopters when they are checking power lines for faults.

It travels along wires strung between pylons and poles across the countryside, and underground through our towns and cities. All these wires are part of a system called the National Grid.

The amount of electricity travelling along the wires is measured in volts. The batteries that produce electricity for your torch or personal stereo probably run at 1.5, 3 or 6 volts. The cables that run between the pylons are 400,000 or 275,000-volt lines.

Power cuts

Have you ever wondered why your electricity suddenly goes off and all the lights go out? Sometimes this happens because somebody digging up a road nearby has cut through an underground cable. Or it can happen when high winds or falling trees break electricity cables. Repairing electrical lines is a dangerous and very skilled job.

POWER POINTS

Transforming electricity

The electricity in the big cables that cross the countryside runs at up to 400,000 volts. But if electricity entered your home at this voltage, all your electrical appliances would blow up! The voltage in your home is set at 230 volts. How is the voltage changed?

A transformer changes the voltage. If you have an electric toy you may have to plug a little box into the wall socket and then plug a thinner wire into your toy. These boxes are transformers. They change the voltage from the 230 volts that comes out of the wall socket to the 6 or 12 volts your toy needs.

In the national network the transformers are in electricity substations. Here the voltage is reduced to the 230 volts that arrives at your home.

Warning!

Transformers can be located on electricity poles or behind fences. There are always warning signs telling you not to touch them. To do so could kill you.

DANGER OF DEATH
KEEP OUT

POWER POINTS

Controlling electricity

Think about how you use electricity in your home. You don't use the same amount all day. You need a lot in the morning, using hot water for washing and making breakfast. Then, when everyone's at school or work, much less is used.

In the evening, when the lights are on, the water heater is on, the cooker is being used, you watch TV, listen to music or turn the computer on, you use the most of all. Then at night, when you are all asleep, you use very little.

Off-peak electricity

Electricity companies charge less for night-time electricity. This is called off-peak electricity or Economy 7. Some meters have separate sets of numbers for daytime and off-peak electricity.

This happens all over the country so the electricity companies have to carefully control how much electricity they generate. Back at the power station people in control rooms decide how much electricity to generate.

Saving electricity

We know that generating electricity can harm our environment. The fossil fuels that we burn in our power stations are running out and they can pollute our air and water.

There are lots of ways to save, or conserve, electricity every day.

• We can switch off lights, radios and televisions when we don't need them.

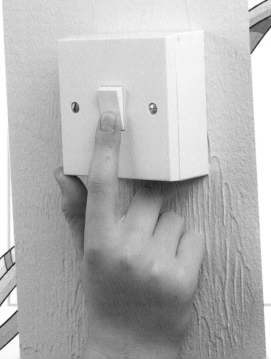

• We can use energy-saving light bulbs which use a quarter of the energy of an ordinary bulb and last ten times longer.

• We can put extra clothes on rather than turn up the electric central heating.

• We can avoid using electric food whisks and tooth brushes, when the job can be done just as easily without.

• We can insulate our lofts to stop heat escaping and have double glazing installed in our windows.

• We can hang our washing on the line to dry instead of using a tumble dryer.

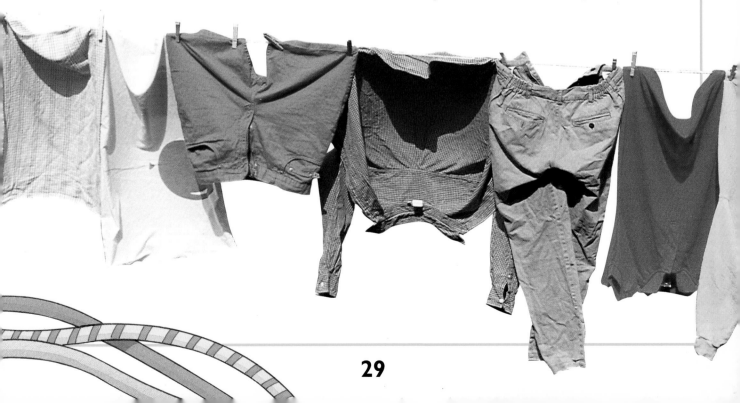

Glossary

Alternative energy Electricity that comes from sources such as the wind and water.

Amber Fossilized resin from extinct trees. When amber is rubbed it becomes electrically charged.

Battery A container or 'cell' in which electrical energy is stored.

Circuit The path along which electricity travels.

Cooling towers The huge towers where steam used to turn turbines is cooled.

Electricity meter A device that measures how much electricity is being used.

Fossil fuels Fuel found in the ground, such as coal and oil, formed from the remains of animals and plants that lived millions of years ago.

Hydro-electric power Electricity made by using water to turn turbines.

Insulator A device or material that prevents electrical wires coming into contact with other wires and with other things.

Main switch The switch that controls the supply of electricity to a building.

Mains electricity Electricity provided by the National Grid.

National Grid The nationwide network of wires and cables that carry electricity around the country.

Power station The huge buildings where electricity is generated.

Pylons The giant metal structures that carry cables around the country.

Renewable energy Energy that comes from a source, such as the wind or the Sun, which does not run out.

Static electricity Electricity created by certain things rubbing together. 'Static' means not moving. Mains electricity moves along cables and wires.

Stored electricity The electricity contained in a battery is called 'stored' electricity.

Substations The places within the National Grid where transformers change the voltage to the right level for supply.

Transformer The device used to change the voltage of electricity.

Turbine A machine with propeller-like blades used to turn the generators that make electricity. Most turbines are turned by the force of steam, wind or water.

Units of electricity Electricity use is measured in units.

Volts The force of the electricity travelling along wires is measured in volts.

Further reading

Ardley, Neil, *Electricity*, Dorling Kindersley, 1998

Bennett, Paul, *What was it like Before Electricity?*, Evans, 1998

De Pinna, Simon, *Electricity*, Wayland, 1997

Good, Keith, *Exciting Electrics*, Evans, 1999

Riley, Peter, *Electricity*, Franklin Watts, 1998

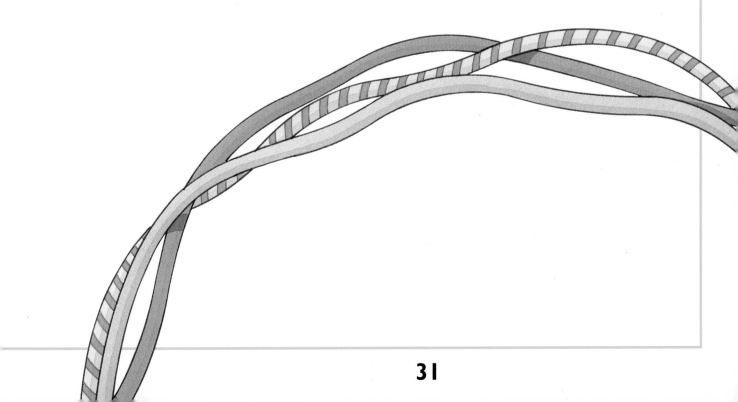

Index